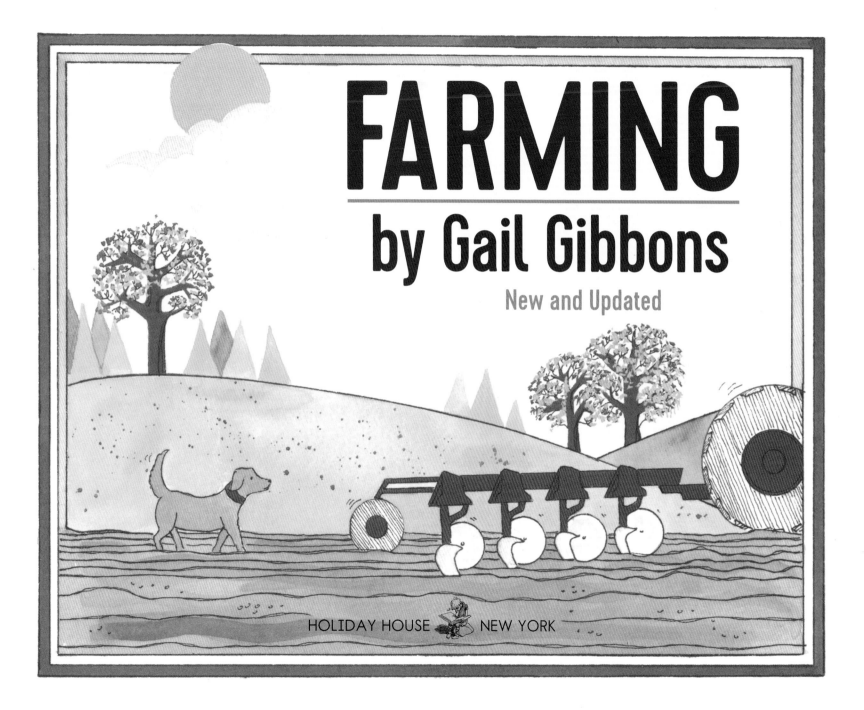

FARMING

by Gail Gibbons

New and Updated

HOLIDAY HOUSE · NEW YORK

Special thanks to Maxine and Gregory Slack
of Corinth, VT; Rudy Martin of M&M Motors,
Montpelier, VT; J. S. Woodhouse Co., West
Springfield, MA; Townline Equipment Sales,
Plainfield, NH; and Kevin Daugherty, Education
Director, Illinois Farm Bureau

Library of Congress Cataloging-in-Publication Data

Gibbons, Gail.
Farming.

Summary: An introduction, in simple text and
illustrations, to farming and the work done on a
farm throughout the seasons.
1. Agriculture — Juvenile literature. 2. Farm life —
Juvenile literature. 3. Farms — Juvenile literature.
[1. Farms. 2. Farm life] I. Title.
S519.G53   1988   630   87-21254

Second Edition
ISBN: 978-0-8234-4276-8 (hardcover)
ISBN: 978-0-8234-4553-0 (paperback)

Farms are where vegetables, fruits, and grains are grown and farm animals are raised.

Some farms are small . . .

others are big.

Most farms are owned by families.
They are busy places throughout the year.

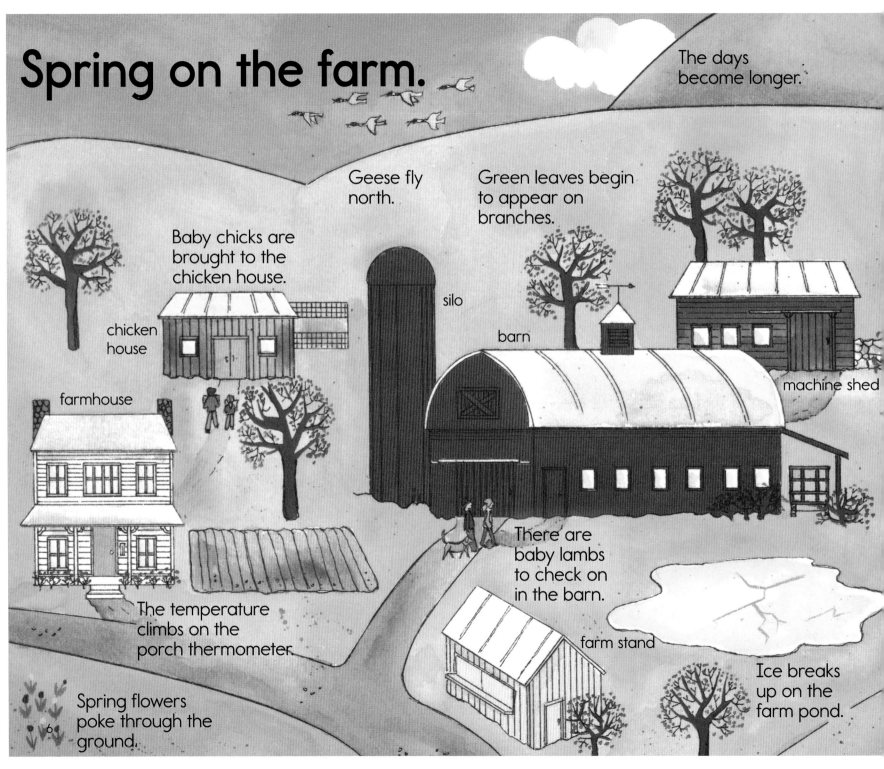

Spring on the farm.

The days become longer.

Geese fly north.

Green leaves begin to appear on branches.

Baby chicks are brought to the chicken house.

silo

chicken house

barn

machine shed

farmhouse

There are baby lambs to check on in the barn.

The temperature climbs on the porch thermometer.

farm stand

Ice breaks up on the farm pond.

Spring flowers poke through the ground.

6

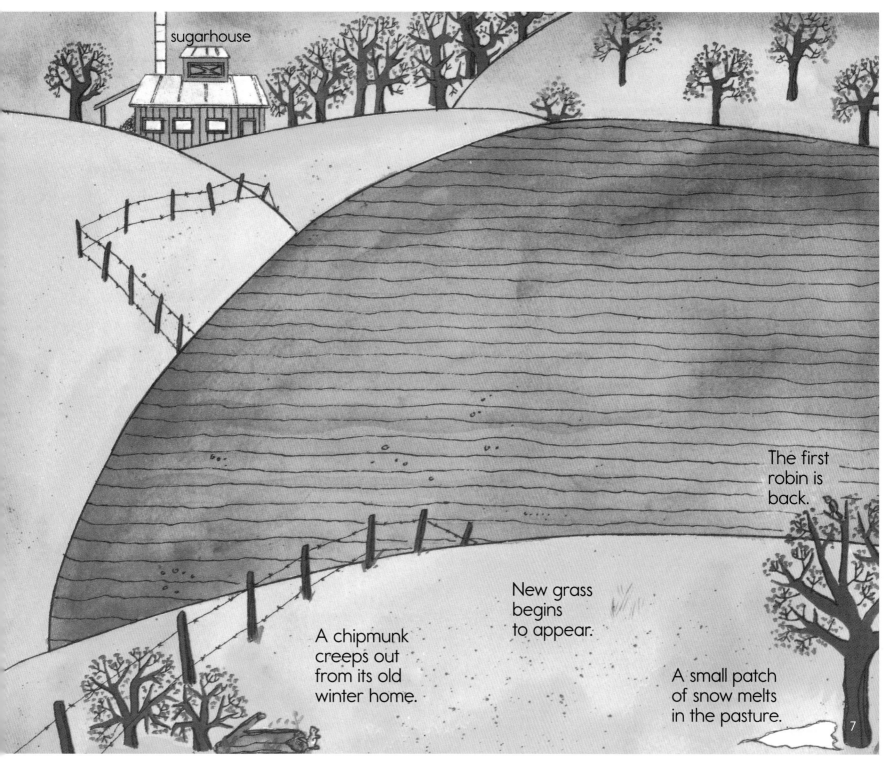

sugarhouse

The first robin is back.

New grass begins to appear.

A chipmunk creeps out from its old winter home.

A small patch of snow melts in the pasture.

7

Outside chores . . .

Horses and cows are put out to pasture.

The vegetable garden is planted.

The maple syrup season has just ended.

Water is lugged to the chicken house.

Fields are fertilized . . .

fertilizer spreader

plowed . . .

The plow turns over the soil.

harrowed . . .

The harrow breaks up and smooths the ground.

and planted.

The planter plants the seeds.

and inside chores.

The stalls are always being cleaned.

The new baby chicks need constant care.

There are new farm babies.

The cows are milked in the morning and in the evening.

Summer on the farm.

It is hot.

beehives

Bees collect nectar from flowers to make honey.

The garden is hoed.

Vegetables grow in the garden.

Time to go swimming!

Flowers bloom.

12

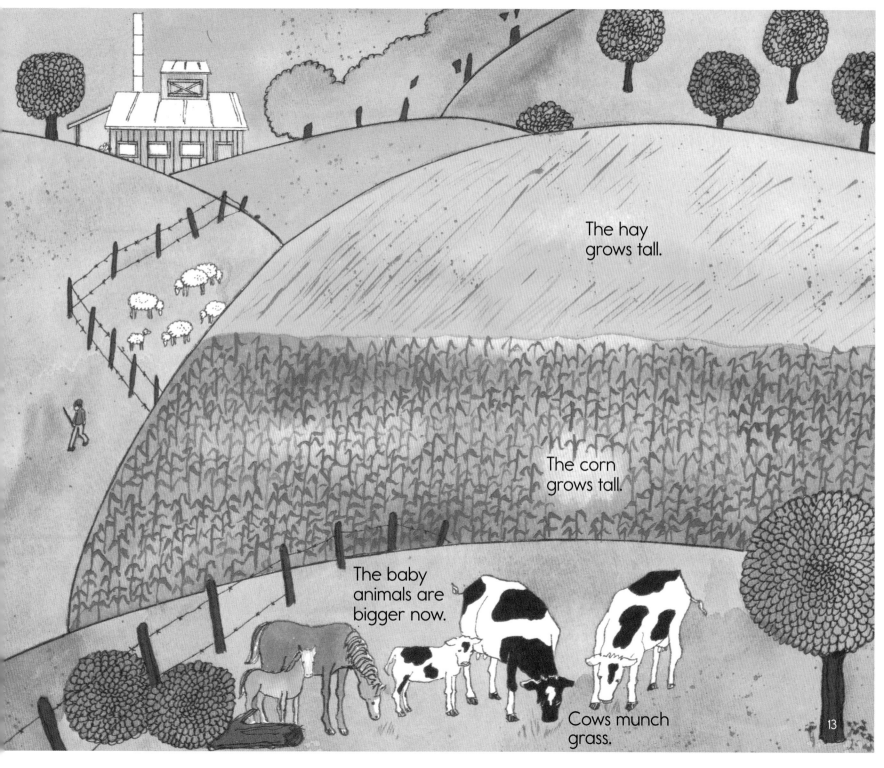

The hay grows tall.

The corn grows tall.

The baby animals are bigger now.

Cows munch grass.

13

Outside chores . . .

Some vegetables are gathered.

Honey is collected.

The hay is mowed . . .

The mower cuts the hay.

tedded . . .

The tedder spreads the hay to dry.

raked . . .

The raker puts the hay in rows.

and baled.

The baler bales the hay.

and inside chores.

Vegetables are canned or frozen.

canning jars

Eggs are collected each day of the year.

The vet gives a calf a checkup.

The cows are milked twice a day every day of the year.

The hay is put in the hayloft.

Fall on the farm.

Geese fly south.

The days become shorter.

The leaves turn gold and orange.

The pumpkins are big and round.

FRESH CORN

18

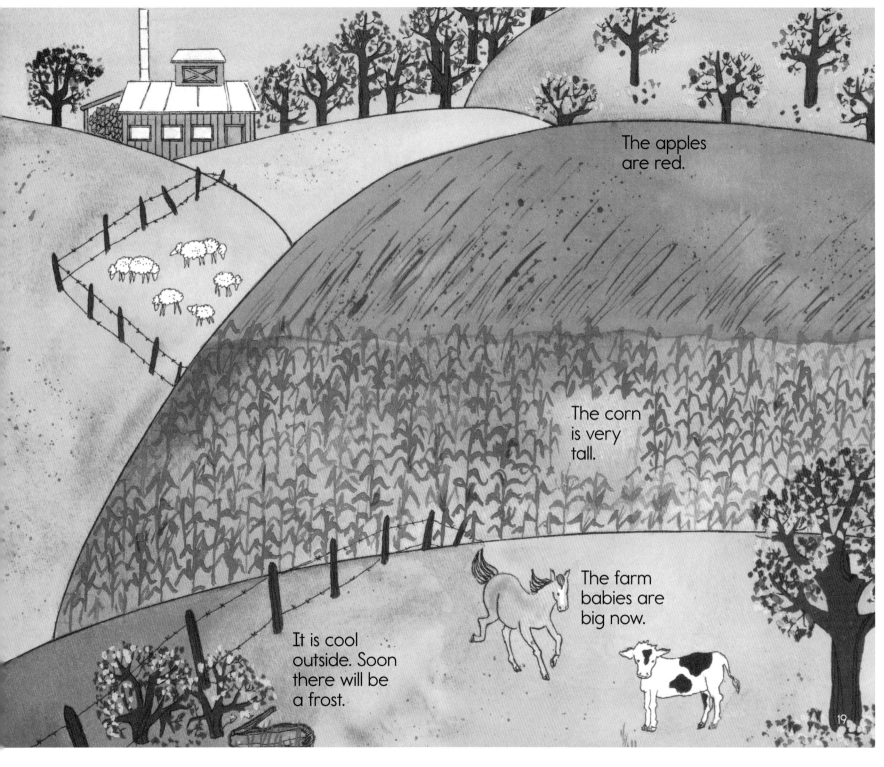

The apples are red.

The corn is very tall.

The farm babies are big now.

It is cool outside. Soon there will be a frost.

Outside chores . . .

After morning chores, it's time to go to school.

Eggs are packed for delivery.

At the end of the growing season, all fruits and vegetables are harvested.

The cornfields
are harvested.

harvester

The silo is filled
with chopped
corn. The corn
and hay will feed
the animals through
the winter.

The hayloft is
packed solid.

and inside chores.

Bushels of apples have been put in the farm stand.

PPLES FOR SALE

Canned foods line the shelves.

ONEY HONEY

Some animals are going to market to be sold.

The cows' milk is sold to a dairy throughout the year.

Winter on the farm.

The days are short.

Footprints lead to the barn.

Ice is on the pond.

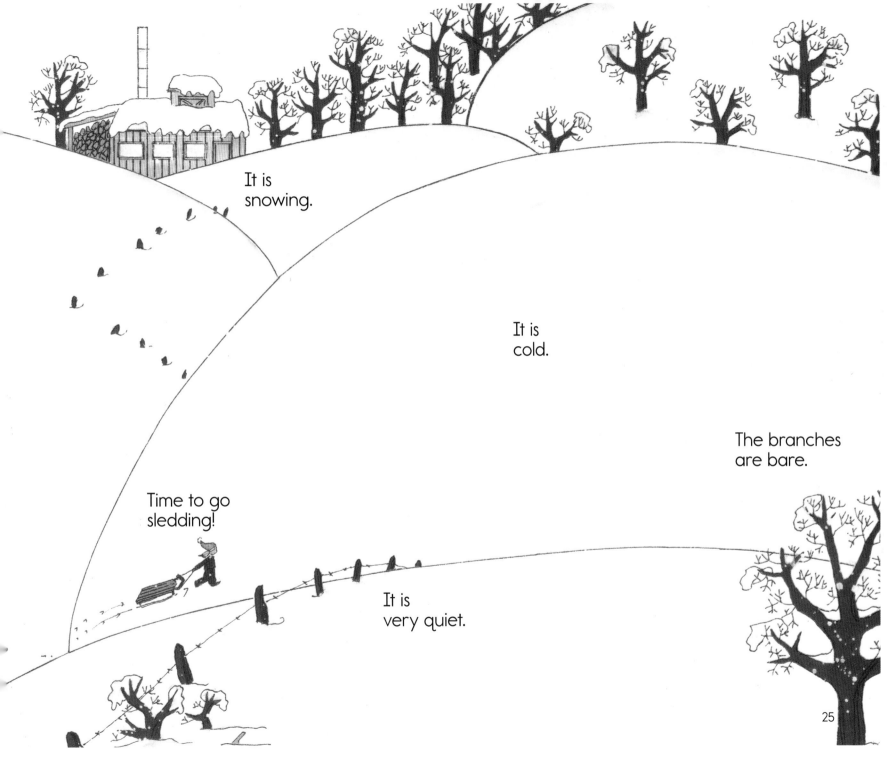

It is
snowing.

It is
cold.

The branches
are bare.

Time to go
sledding!

It is
very quiet.

25

Outside chores . . .

The road
is plowed.

Water is
carried to
the chicken
house.

and inside chores.

Farm machinery is repaired and cleaned.

The cows are milked.

There is plenty of hay and grain to eat.

All the animals are inside for the cold winter.

Last summer's vegetables simmer in a pot.

Bookkeeping and plans for next year's crops are worked on.

In winter
everyone goes
to bed early.

Soon spring
will come
again.

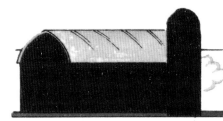

KINDS OF FARMING

Most farms are specialized. They produce one or two main crops or kinds of farm animals.

DAIRY FARMS

Dairy farms raise dairy cows for their milk. The milk is sold to dairies where it is processed and packaged.

EGG AND POULTRY FARMS

Egg farms raise chickens to lay eggs. Poultry farms raise chickens for their meat.

GRAIN FARMS

Grain farms grow grain for making bread and cereals and other foods. Some grains are grown for animals, too.

FRUIT FARMS

Fruit farms grow apples, peaches, oranges, and other fruits for people to eat.

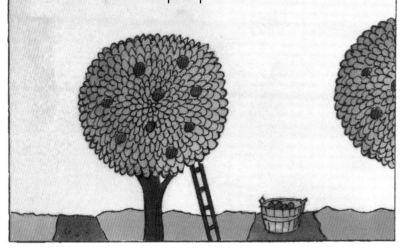

VEGETABLE FARMS

Vegetable farms grow beans, lettuce, carrots, and other vegetables. They are sent to market and stores to be sold.

CATTLE FARMS AND RANCHES

Beef cattle, pigs, and other animals are raised for their meat.

FARMING . . .

Many people like to buy their produce from the thousands of farmers' markets across the United States, which sell food grown on local farms.

Buying locally grown food saves energy because the food doesn't have to travel long distances by planes and trucks.

The more recently picked a fruit or vegetable is, the more vitamins and nutrients it has.

Local farms are more likely to grow heirloom fruits and vegetables.

Heirloom crops come from seeds that have been protected and carefully cultivated through many generations. There have been no chemicals added or changes made to these seeds.

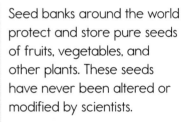

Seed banks around the world protect and store pure seeds of fruits, vegetables, and other plants. These seeds have never been altered or modified by scientists.

Heirloom produce is more nutritious and comes in more varieties than regular fruits and vegetables. It also tends to be juicier and have more flavor.

Many farmers use genetically modified organism (GMO) seeds. These seeds are altered by scientists to create new varieties and to increase sizes of crops.